Voices for Freedom
Abolitionist Heroes

BY SUSAN
BROPHY DOWN

THEODORE WELD

Architect of Abolitionism

CRABTREE
Publishing Company
www.crabtreebooks.com

CRABTREE Publishing Company
www.crabtreebooks.com

Photographs and reproductions:
Alamy: page 9 (top), page 27, page 48, page 60. Creative Commons: page 9 (bottom), page 12, page 20 (bottom). Courtesy of Documenting the American South, The University of North Carolina at Chapel Hill Libraries: page 11, page 62. The Granger Collection: page 18, page 34 (top), page 46 (bottom), page 50 (bottom). Courtesy of the Library of Congress/public domain: cover (all), page 1, page 3, page 4 (both), page 5, page 6, page 7, page 8 (top), page 10, page 12 (both), page 14, page 15 (both), page 16 (both), page 17 (both), page 19 (both), page 20 (top), page 23, page 24 (both), page 26, page 28 (bottom), page 29 (both), page 30 (both), page 31, page 33 (both), page 34 (bottom), page 35, page 36 (both), page 38 (both), page 40 (both), page 42, page 43 (both), page 44 (bottom), page 46 (top), page 47, page 49, page 50 (top), page 51, page 52, page 53, page 54, page 55 (all), page 57, page 58, page 61. Shutterstock: page 8 (bottom), page 22, page 28 (top), page 41 (bottom), page 44 (top).

Front cover (inset), back cover, title page, page 3: An engraving of Theodore Weld, from around 1844. **Front Cover (top):** A photograph of African-American slaves standing in front of slave quarters, sometime during the mid-1800s. **Bottom:** A series of anti-slavery trading cards from the 1800s, by American artist Henry Louis Stephens. Pictures like this were used by abolitionists to convince people that slavery should be stopped.

Author: Susan Brophy Down
Publishing plan research and development:
Sean Charlebois, Reagan Miller
Crabtree Publishing Company
Project coordinator: Mark Sachner,
Water Buffalo Books
Editors: Mark Sachner, Lynn Peppas
Proofreader: Wendy Scavuzzo
Editorial director: Kathy Middleton
Photo researchers: Ruth Owen, Mark Sachner
Designer: Westgraphix/Tammy West
Cover design: Katherine Berti
Indexer: Gini Holland
Production coordinator: Margaret Amy Salter
Print coordinators: Margaret Amy Salter and Katherine Berti
Prepress technician: Margaret Amy Salter
Editorial consultant: James Marten, Ph.D.; Chair,
Department of History, Marquette University

Written, developed, and produced by
Water Buffalo Books

Publisher's note:
All quotations in this book come from original sources and contain the spelling and grammatical inconsistencies of the original text. Some of the quotations may also contain terms that are no longer in use and may be considered inappropriate or offensive. The use of such terms is for the sake of preserving the historical and literary accuracy of the sources and should not be seen as encouraging or endorsing the use of such terms today.

Library and Archives Canada Cataloguing in Publication

Down, Susan Brophy
Theodore Weld : architect of abolitionism / Susan Brophy Down.

(Voices for freedom: abolitionist heroes)
Includes index.
Issued also in electronic format.
ISBN 978-0-7787-1065-3 (pbk.).--ISBN 978-0-7787-1062-2 (bound)

1. Weld, Theodore Dwight, 1803-1895--Juvenile literature. 2. Abolitionists--United States--Biography--Juvenile literature. 3. Anti-slavery movements--United States--History--19th century--Juvenile literature. I. Title. II. Series: Voices for freedom: abolitionist heroes

E449.W46D69 2013   j326'.8092   C2013-901034-3

Library of Congress Cataloging-in-Publication Data

Down, Susan Brophy.
Theodore Weld : architect of abolitionism / Susan Brophy Down.
pages cm. -- (Voices for freedom : abolitionist heroes)
Includes index.
ISBN 978-0-7787-1062-2 (reinforced library binding) -- ISBN 978-0-7787-1065-3 (pbk.) -- ISBN 978-1-4271-9311-7 (electronic pdf) -- ISBN 978-1-4271-9235-6 (electronic html)
1. Weld, Theodore Dwight, 1803-1895--Juvenile literature. 2. Abolitionists--United States--Biography--Juvenile literature. 3. Social reformers--United States--Biography--Juvenile literature. 4. Antislavery movements--United States--History--19th century--Juvenile literature. I. Title.

E449.W46D69 2013
326.092--dc23
[B]
                              2013004912

Crabtree Publishing Company
www.crabtreebooks.com   1-800-387-7650

Printed in the U.S.A./042013/SX20130306

Published in Canada
Crabtree Publishing
616 Welland Ave.
St. Catharines, Ontario
L2M 5V6

Published in the United States
Crabtree Publishing
PMB 59051
350 Fifth Ave., Suite 3308
New York, NY 10118

Published in the United Kingdom
Crabtree Publishing
Maritime House
Basin Road North, Hove
BN41 1WR

Published in Australia
Crabtree Publishing
3 Charles Street
Coburg North
VIC, 3058

Contents

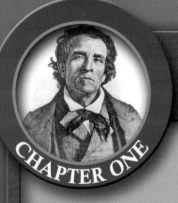

CHAPTER ONE

Threatened but Unbroken

I t was a chilly February in 1835 in Circleville, Ohio. Inside a local church, Theodore Dwight Weld was making another fiery speech about why African Americans should be freed from slavery. With his wild, unkempt hair and his thundering voice, Weld was an unforgettable speaker who dazzled his listeners. After he talked about the terrible condition of slaves on Southern plantations, Weld convinced many in his audience to join the anti-slavery cause.

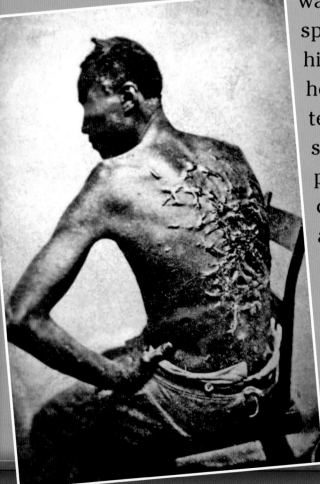

This photograph, taken in 1863, shows the scars on the back of a slave who was repeatedly subjected to brutal whippings by an overseer in Baton Rouge, Louisiana.

This wood engraving shows a pro-slavery riot in Alton, Illinois, that was typical of many acts of violence against abolitionists in Northern states. This raid, which occurred in 1837, was on a warehouse containing the printing press and anti-slavery publications of Elijah Parish Lovejoy. Lovejoy, an abolitionist minister, journalist, and publisher, was murdered during the attack.

"The Most-Mobbed Man"

Ohio had banned slavery in its constitution in 1802, but many white Ohioans were still prejudiced against African Americans. Whites who had recently moved to Ohio feared that freed slaves would come and take their jobs or their land. As early as 1804, the state passed a series of laws that aimed to discourage African Americans from settling in Ohio. These laws, known as black laws, forced African-American residents to show a certificate of freedom; post a legal agreement, called a bond, promising good behavior; and pay a fee to the county in which they lived. At the time, the laws also prevented their children from attending school, although this portion of the law was changed in 1853.

It is hardly surprising that, backed by a tradition including these and other forms of discrimination, many in the crowd disagreed with Weld. Nor is it surprising that he became a target for their violent reactions. Suddenly, Weld was hit by a rock thrown through the window of the church where he was speaking. Dazed, he had to pause for a few minutes before he started talking again. He didn't want to quit, despite the dangers he regularly faced in his travels across the wild, young country.

Slavery—A Terrible History

Slavery is a system in which human beings are bought, sold, and forced to work for others. This terrible practice has occurred throughout human history, and in most parts of the world. In the early 1500s, on Caribbean islands such as Cuba and Hispaniola, Spain became the first European country to use African slaves in the Americas. Portugal, Britain, and France also participated in what is known as the Atlantic slave trade. These nations forcibly removed Africans from their homelands to colonies in North, Central, and South America, and the Caribbean.

When the United States became an independent nation in the late 1700s, the new states created their own laws. Many Northern states banned slavery, beginning with Vermont in 1777. In 1807, the British government banned the slave trade throughout the British Empire. In 1808, the U.S. government did the same. The new law did not, however, prohibit people from owning, buying, and selling slaves they already possessed—or the children of those slaves—particularly in the Southern states. Over time, differences of opinion over slavery deepened between Northern and Southern states, and the issue of slavery became one of the underlying causes—and eventually the principal issue—of the Civil War (1861–1865).

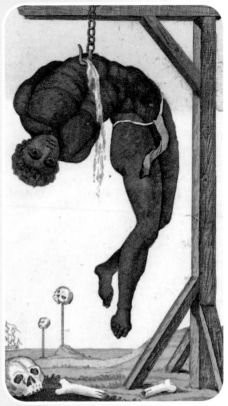

An engraving by English poet, artist, and printer William Blake entitled "A Negro Hung Alive by the Ribs to a Gallows." The print first appeared in a narrative, published in 1796, by John Gabriel Stedman, a British-Dutch sailor and author. Stedman's firsthand account of his experiences with slavery and slaves in Surinam, South America, contained many descriptions of extreme cruelty. The narrative and its illustrations were based mostly on Stedman's personal observations. They became tools used by abolitionists in their campaign against slavery in the United States.

The next night, Weld had to find a different place where he could deliver his speech to more people. The church organizers were afraid that angry mobs might damage the building. Their fears were justified. As Weld spoke the next night, he heard stones and clubs rattling against the shutters from outside. When he left the building afterward, he was greeted by a hostile mob with nails, eggs, and stones to throw at him.

Night after night, in many different cities, Weld converted people to his anti-slavery cause after they heard his speeches. He also faced the wrath of violent opponents. Angry reactions reached a point that Weld eventually was nicknamed "the most-mobbed man in the United States."

Backlash Against Freedom

At the time of Weld's speech against slavery, the economy of the American South was based on plantations growing tobacco and cotton, and a large slave population to make those plantations profitable. Most Southern plantation owners and politicians justified slavery in various ways. One way was to claim that the system was actually good for the slaves because it provided them with food and shelter, organized their labor, and led them to Christianity.

In his lectures and writings, Weld demonstrated that the life of a slave was harsh and violent. His most famous contribution to the anti-slavery movement was his 1839 book

A photo, taken around 1862, of a group of African-American slaves planting sweet potatoes on a plantation in South Carolina. Some of the slaves hoe and plow the ground, while others cut piles of sweet potatoes for planting.

Slaves toil on a Southern plantation. Conditions for field hands were harsh. Slaves usually picked cotton with their bare hands in the blazing sun from sunrise to sundown six days a week, with little food or water.

American Slavery As It Is: Testimony of a Thousand Witnesses. The book includes excerpts from newspaper reports and collected narratives from ministers and other respected people who had seen what slaves had to endure. This factual approach was difficult for slave owners to argue against.

Economic self-interest was also the reason many Northern business owners were reluctant to see slaves freed. Even though owning slaves was illegal in those states, business owners relied on cheap cotton and other goods for their factories. Meanwhile, Northern laborers and factory workers worried that freed slaves would come North and take their jobs.

A Point to Ponder

"We hold these Truths to be self-evident, that all Men are created equal, that they are endowed by their Creator with certain unalienable Rights, that among these are Life, Liberty, and the Pursuit of Happiness."

These famous lines are from the United States Declaration of Independence, signed in 1776. The document represented the Thirteen Colonies' break with Great Britain at the end of the Revolutionary War. Although the Declaration was not a law, it was considered a moral code of American beliefs. Passages such as the one quoted here have inspired other countries and movements for women's rights and civil rights. Anti-slavery activists argued that it was hypocritical to agree with the Declaration that "all men are created equal" and yet believe that African Americans were merely pieces of property, not people.

A slave is forced by his white overseer to brutally whip another slave. In his writings, Theodore Weld used accounts of incidents like this one, which took place in Virginia before the start of the Civil War, to make his case for the abolition of slavery.

> *Slaveholders are always talking of their kind treatment of their slaves... Despots always insist that they are merciful.*

– from *American Slavery As It Is: Testimony of a Thousand Witnesses*, by Theodore Weld

Cotton and Slavery

Cotton grown in America was full of seeds and husks. These had to be removed before the cotton could be made into cloth. Cleaning the cotton by hand took so long that the crop was barely worth growing. In 1793, U.S. inventor Eli Whitney built a machine that could quickly clean cotton. It was called the cotton "gin"—short for "engine." It allowed cotton to be grown profitably all across the South. The cotton gin increased the demand for cotton plantations, and that increased the demand for slaves.

This photo, taken in Alabama in 1923, shows a community cotton gin. It is similar to those used to further the cotton trade in the 1800s and, along with it, the South's dependence on cotton and the slaves who picked it. One huge difference between this scene and what it might have looked like in the 1800s: This gin was owned and operated by the African Americans who are shown in the photo.

Africans kidnapped into slavery suffered horribly cramped conditions on their voyages to America. In this engraving, men are shown crowded onto the deck of a ship. Behind them, on an upper deck, are female slaves.

A Gradual Shift

The U.S. Constitution, the supreme law of the United States, was drafted in 1787. The Constitution imposed a 20-year waiting period before a ban on the slave trade could be considered. At the time, many people believed that the practice of slavery would gradually decline on its own. Slavery continued to become more and more profitable, however, and slave owners became more powerful. During the ten years before the slave trade was ended in 1808, slave traders were busier than ever. More than 200,000 new slaves were forcibly taken from their homes in Africa, put in chains, and crammed together for weeks on end below the decks of the notorious slave ships that took them to America.

While politicians were arguing about how and whether to end slavery, the slave population continued to grow. By 1810, there were more than one million slaves in the United States. In some Southern states, more than half the population consisted of slaves. In South Carolina, two-thirds

The Three-Fifths Compromise of 1787

How many people should be elected to Congress from each state? That depends on the population of each state. When the rules were written into the U.S. Constitution, Southerners argued that slaves should be counted among those represented in Congress, even though slaves had none of the rights of people who were free. The North disagreed, so the writers of the Constitution decided a slave would be counted as three-fifths of a person. For every five slaves, three persons were added to the population. This meant that slave states, nearly all of which were in the South, had more votes and power in the House of Representatives than if only white people were counted.

of the state's people were slaves. White slave owners were afraid of what would happen if the black population became free. If, for example, slaves were allowed to learn to read and write, many whites feared slaves would read literature that would convince them to turn against their masters.

Slavery became the central issue that would turn the North against the South in the Civil War (1861–1865). In the years leading up to that epic battle, Weld and others opposed to slavery, known as abolitionists, were bravely fighting on their own to support equality and freedom for all people—black and white alike. Some abolitionists believed that slavery was a sin and a crime, and they pushed for its immediate end. Some argued for violent resistance to slavery, while others were willing to consider more gradual change. Weld's group didn't want a violent change through slave rebellion or a war between the states. Like most abolitionists, their goal was to convince people to free their slaves.

Widely Read

Weld's efforts to convince people of the evils of slavery made him one of the greatest voices in the abolitionist movement. As a lecturer and a writer, he swayed many people over to his side, even as he courageously spoke out in support of beliefs that were unpopular. He traveled the country to reach out to new audiences. Even when, over the years, he worked so hard that his voice gave out, he did valuable research for politicians who wanted to change the laws.

Weld's greatest literary work, *American Slavery As It Is: Testimony of a Thousand Witnesses* (shown here), was one of the most widely read abolitionist books of its time. It continues to be a massive resource providing documented examples of the cruel treatment of one group of humans by another. In its day, it also inspired other writers to raise their voices, as well as their pens, against slavery.

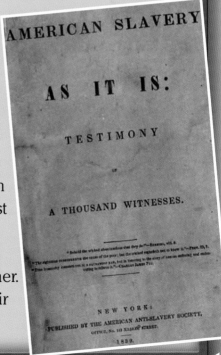

CHAPTER TWO

Choosing to Travel the Righteous Path

Born in Hampton, Connecticut, on November 23, 1803, Theodore Dwight Weld was part of a large and influential family. His father Ludovicus was a Harvard graduate, and both his father and grandfather were Congregational ministers. Young Weld was a gifted child who started school at the age of three and inherited his family's gift for public speaking, as well as its strict moral code.

This illustration shows an anguished slave in chains and bears the motto "Am I not a man and a brother?" Originally the seal of the Society for the Abolition of Slavery in Britain during the late 1700s, it became a commonly used emblem for abolitionists on both sides of the Atlantic.

The American School for the Deaf, founded in 1817 in Hartford, Connecticut, is a pioneering school in the educating of people who are deaf or have other types of hearing loss. Theodore Weld's brother Lewis was associated with the school from its beginnings, both as a teacher and the school's principal, until shortly before his death in 1853.

A Tornado of a Boyhood

Weld was known as Thoda by his large and boisterous family. He was the fourth child with three older brothers: Lewis (1796), Charles (1799), Ezra (1801), and a younger sister, Cornelia Elizabeth (1809). As adults, his siblings pursued different careers: one brother became a minister, another taught at what is now the American School for the Deaf in West Hartford, Connecticut, and another became a famous daguerreotype photographer.

Weld was rambunctious as a child. During his romps in the countryside, he suffered several broken bones and dislocated joints. Even after he grew up, he told his future wife that he still liked to "jump and hop and scream like a loon and run on all fours and wrestle and throw stones." The active boy also took the time to be kind and compassionate. One day at school, he watched the teacher tell a new African-American student in his classroom that he should sit apart from the other students. Weld decided to move his chair to sit next to the student, which made the other students tease him as well as the black student. Weld's commitment to combating prejudice would inspire him to make similar gestures throughout his life.

By the time Weld was born, slavery was a controversial subject. Weld was just a child when Britain and the United States abolished the slave trade. Unfortunately, in the United States, this only restricted importing new

The Accomplished Weld Family

The Weld family has been a major influence in politics, education, and business in Boston and the New England states since the 17th century, when the three Weld brothers (Thomas, Daniel, and Joseph) emigrated from England. In 1650, Thomas's son Edmund was the first Weld to graduate from Harvard University. There are now about 20 Harvard graduates from the Weld family. Joseph became an army captain and a military hero during the Pequot War of 1637. He later received a land grant for what is now Jamaica Plain, part of Boston. Another Weld amassed a fleet of clipper ships that traded with Asia. The wealthy Welds are known for their acts of generosity and have made major donations to Harvard, the Massachusetts Institute of Technology (MIT), and other recipients.

When actress Tuesday Weld, shown here around 1960, played Thalia Menninger on CBS's *The Many Loves of Doby Gillis*, few people knew that she was a member of the distinguished New England Weld family.

Famous contemporary family members include former Massachusetts governor William Floyd Weld (1991–1997) and Hollywood actress Tuesday Weld, who is probably best known for the role she played in 1959 on the CBS situation comedy *The Many Loves of Dobie Gillis*.

slaves from Africa. It did not free the slaves already toiling in the United States. In fact, it made them more valuable, and the buying and selling of slaves continued. By 1840, the slave population in the United States had increased to 2.5 million.

Weld was expected to become a minister, like his father and grandfather. To finish his high school studies, he was sent to Phillips Andover Academy, a highly regarded private boarding school. He attended for only a short time before the stress of studying caused him to go temporarily blind. He was forced to leave school and return home to recover.

A Way with Words

After a few months of rest, Weld's eyesight returned. His doctor suggested that travel would be good for him rather than more school. His family couldn't afford to send him away, so he raised money for his journeys by working as he traveled. He decided he could earn money by giving a series of lectures on mnemonics—the science of memory. These were lessons he had learned from a teacher at his last school. The lectures were extremely popular, and they gave him practice in public speaking. The experience would later give him a valuable advantage when he preached against slavery. During his travels in the South, he witnessed the slave economy for the first time, which deeply troubled him. He saw the way slaves were oppressed and had to live by unfair laws known as slave codes.

Theodore Weld spent much of his childhood playing in the countryside around his home in Connecticut. In this photo, bison graze on a farm in Windham County, near Hampton, the peaceful and picturesque town in which Weld was born.

Meanwhile, Weld's parents had moved to a small farm in New York state. When he returned from his travels, he attended Hamilton College, which wasn't far from where his parents lived. It was in upstate New York that Weld met people who would influence his thinking and help shape both his passion for reform and his future.

Pearson Hall is one of the oldest buildings at Phillips Academy in Andover, Massachusetts. It was built in 1818—the year before Theodore Weld attended school there.

15

Two views of slave pens from the 1800s in Alexandria, Virginia, where slaves were held and kept in miserable conditions while they waited to be put up for auction. In the exterior view, soldiers are shown outside a pen, probably at a point during the Civil War when Union troops occupied parts of Virginia.

Slave Codes

Slave codes were state laws governing the rights of slave owners and the status of their slaves. These laws, passed mostly in Southern states from the mid-1600s through the early 1700s, severely restricted slaves' lives.

For example, slaves could not leave their masters' homes without permission, wear fine clothes, or associate with free blacks or white people in their homes. They were severely punished for any infractions. Slaves could not fight against masters, even in self-defense. If they did they faced death, while the law allowed their masters to kill them without penalty. In some states, white people could be fined if they taught a slave to read and write.

Charles Finney: A Dynamic Spiritual Presence

Weld was reaching adulthood during a period known as the Second Great Awakening. This was a time when new Christian religious movements were spread by traveling preachers who delivered persuasive talks to local residents. Many Americans were hungry for a new type of religion, one with less ritual and rigid ceremony than that of the conservative Protestant churches of the day. Evangelical speakers such as Charles Finney (1792–1875) opened their arms to everyone. Finney preached immediate salvation for people who accepted Jesus and

Hamilton College, in Clinton, New York, one of the nation's top liberal arts colleges. Theodore Weld studied for a time here, starting in 1824.

promised to do good works. He wasn't a trained minister, and his meetings weren't like church at all. His sermons were often directed at individual members of the church, and his words caused emotional reactions among listeners.

Weld had heard about Finney and his lively meetings, known as revivals, where people shouted and crowded around the speaker. Weld was loyal to his father's traditional brand of religion, however, and he was critical of Finney's message and his methods of preaching. Finally, Weld's Aunt Sophia brought him along to her church when she knew that Finney would be speaking.

The preacher had heard about Weld's criticism of him. Weld had told many of his fellow students at Hamilton College that Finney's tactics were wrong because he encouraged people to reject traditional churches and their rituals. Finney's sermon was called "One Sinner Destroyeth Much Good," and as he spoke, he stared straight at young Weld. Weld's aunt had seated him in the middle of the row, so he couldn't escape. "[Finney] just held me up on his toasting-fork before that audience," Weld remembered.

Charles Finney, an energetic and magnetic preacher, was one of the first—and most powerful—influences on Theodore Weld's moral character. Finney was an early supporter of the abolitionist movement, but he and Weld often disagreed on matters concerning religion and spirituality.

17

Weld was furious at being forced to listen to the preacher. When he happened to meet Finney the following day in a shop in town, Weld ranted at him in front of a crowd of people. He later visited Finney's home to apologize for his rudeness. He then spent a sleepless night wondering if perhaps Finney had the right idea after all. Weld finally underwent a spiritual conversion, or change, in which he accepted Finney's belief that salvation was possible for anyone who accepted Jesus and did good works. He left his studies at Hamilton College to become one of Finney's group of preachers, known as the Holy Band. As a result, he was back on the road again doing what he excelled at and enjoyed—speaking to groups about the things he was passionate about.

At first, Weld spoke about his newfound spiritual beliefs. He also preached that those he converted to his beliefs must use their reawakened morality for good causes. Temperance—the control of alcohol—was one of the causes that Weld preached about in his early lectures. Many considered excessive drinking to be the cause of immoral behavior, crime, and family violence. Over time, his passion became the abolitionist cause, and his message would be directed at the evils of slavery.

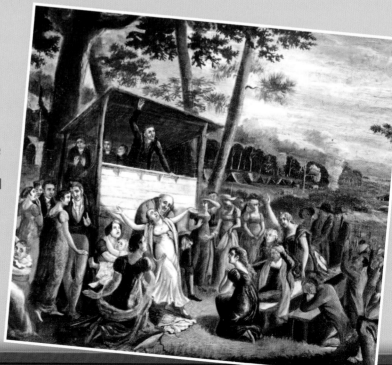

This oil painting by American artist Jeremiah Paul captures the spirit, intensity, and powerful feeling of a 19th-century Christian revival meeting. The participants, urged by the preacher to come forward, are generally in a state of emotional and spiritual excitement. Some are on their feet offering up their prayers and praising God, while others kneel or are overcome with emotion. Only a few around the edges of the crowd appear not to be caught up in the spirit of the revival.

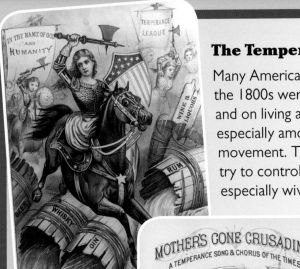

The Temperance Movement

Many American social reform movements of the 1800s were part of a new focus on religion and on living a moral life. One popular cause, especially among women, was the temperance movement. This was an attempt to stop, or try to control, alcohol consumption. Women, especially wives and mothers who had been hurt by men's uncontrolled drinking, were the most active temperance workers. The American Temperance Society was established in 1826.

Pressure on the government led to the ratification, or approval, in 1919 of the Eighteenth Amendment to the U.S. Constitution, which prohibited the manufacture and sale of alcohol. The era known as Prohibition, which lasted from 1920 to 1933, did not achieve the goals of the temperance movement. Local governments and police did little to enforce the law, especially in large cities. The federal government assigned a limited number of agents to combat the smuggling, or bootlegging, of alcohol into the country, much of it by members of organized crime. Prohibition was finally repealed, or reversed, by the Twenty-first Amendment to the Constitution, which placed the enacting and enforcing of anti-liquor laws into the hands of state governments.

Two views of temperance as expressed in popular culture in the 1800s. The political cartoon titled "Women's Holy War" (above) connects the campaign against alcohol with patriotism, social responsibility, and women's issues. The heroine on horseback, holding a shield with an emblem based on the American flag, leads an army of women breaking apart barrels containing alcoholic beverages. The other image (right) is of sheet music entitled "Mother's Gone Crusading." The illustration criticizes wives and mothers for leaving their husbands and children to fend for themselves at home while the women attend temperance rallies.

CHAPTER THREE

The Power of Ideas

Charles Finney's Holy Band of preachers, which included Theodore Weld, conducted so many religious revival meetings that Finney referred to some parts of New York state as the "burned over district." This meant that almost everyone had been converted already and there were no more potential recruits to fuel the religious fire. Weld, meanwhile, had his own reasons for moving on from his role as an evangelical preacher. In 1827, he gave up speaking

at revivals. He was forming stronger opinions about slavery, and he preferred to lecture about abolitionism than to preach about religion. Finney didn't agree, believing that Weld should concentrate on spiritual subjects. For Weld, it was time to go back to school. There, his values would take shape in an atmosphere where ideas were freely exchanged.

Charles Stuart: Nurturing a Newfound Passion

Weld had learned about the power of ideas when he traveled about with Finney, preaching in small towns. Now he wanted to finish his education and, in 1827, he chose the Oneida Institute in Whitestown, New York, where he studied for three years. Oneida was a manual labor training college. In addition to reading books and doing lessons, the students were required to do several hours of manual labor every day in exchange for tuition and room and board. Weld loved the idea. He was responsible for 30 cows, and he had to get out of bed at 4:00 A.M. to milk them.

This memorial to slaves sits on a site where slave auctions were once held in Zanzibar, which is now part of Tanzania in Africa. The sculpture depicts the horrific reality of the African slave trade—an entire family, captured by slavers and placed in a holding cell, chained and manacled, soon to be sold in some other part of the world. In this view of the sculpture, water fills part of the holding cell. At other times, the chains are rearranged so one member of the family is unchained. This dramatizes the hopelessness of families being forever separated and torn apart. Descriptions of scenes like this, along with eyewitness accounts coming from the docks and slave markets of cities throughout the United States, fueled the dedication of abolitionists like Theodore Weld to the anti-slavery cause.

A scene similar to what greeted Theodore Weld every day during his time at the Oneida Institute—dairy cows grazing on farmland in upstate New York.

While he was studying, Weld met Captain Charles Stuart, a British-born man who lived in Canada. There, Stuart supported a community of African-American refugees. Stuart was a warm-hearted person who helped Weld with his college tuition and became something of a father figure to him. He was also the first to convince Weld to become an anti-slavery activist. When Stuart moved back to Britain for a short time, he sent Weld pamphlets from the anti-slavery society there.

Taking Up the Cause: The Tappan Brothers

While studying at Oneida, Weld met Lewis Tappan, a wealthy businessman who had sent his sons to study at the college. Lewis and his brother Arthur were philanthropists and wanted to support worthwhile causes. They also liked the idea that hard physical work was just as important as academic study. They formed the Society for Manual Labor, and they hired Weld to travel the country and give lectures on the topic.

Dangerous Journeys

Traveling even a short distance was difficult and uncomfortable in the early 1830s. Steam locomotives were new and rare, and very little railroad track existed. To get from town to town, Weld walked, rode on horseback, or took a stagecoach. He estimated he traveled 4,500 miles (7,242 km) in a year, and he made 236 public addresses on topics of moral reform. Along the way, he suffered some mishaps. In Connecticut, a drunk driver ran his stagecoach off the road so that it flipped over, causing a wild jumble of broken harnesses, bruised and hysterical passengers, and luggage that was strewn about on the ground. Weld had to recuperate for several weeks because of a sprained wrist and head injury.

In 1840, Anglo-Canadian abolitionist Charles Stuart attended the World Anti-Slavery Convention in London. The meeting drew thousands of abolitionists from around the globe, including several freed slaves and female delegates. Having women present was itself a controversial move, even among female abolitionists. In this painting of the convention by Benjamin Robert Haydon, Charles Stuart's face is circled.

Abolitionist Heroes

Charles Stuart (1783–1865) helped former slaves start new lives as farmers in Upper Canada (now a part of Ontario). Born in Jamaica to Scottish parents, he had a military career before moving to North America. While working at a school in New York, he met young Theodore Weld and they became lifelong friends, going on lecture tours together for the anti-slavery cause. Stuart later moved back to Canada and worked for other causes. These included temperance (anti-alcohol) and helping feed people who were starving during a severe food shortage, or famine, in Ireland. Meanwhile, in his own home, he refused to have any goods made by slaves.

Abolitionist Heroes

Arthur Tappan (1786–1865) and **Lewis Tappan** (1788–1873) were brothers who used their wealth to support the abolitionist cause. Born in Massachusetts, they later moved to New York City, where they created a number of successful businesses such as silk importing, publishing, and financial services. They funded schools and also founded, with William Lloyd Garrison, the American Anti-Slavery Society (AASS), of which Arthur became the first president. They resigned from the AASS over their disagreement with the society's support of women's rights, and formed the American and Foreign Anti-Slavery Society.

In 1841, a group of Africans who were kidnapped as slaves had taken over the ship *Amistad* on which they were being transported. The Tappans supported the Africans while their case was being heard by the United States Supreme Court. Lewis took a particular interest in the case. The Tappans later supported new churches and founded the American Missionary Association, which aided escaped slaves. After the Civil War, they supported new colleges for freed slaves.

Lewis (left) and Arthur Tappan were ardent supporters of the abolitionist cause, even when their views earned them the open hostility of people who opposed them. When the government enacted laws that punished those who were working to free slaves, the brothers used their wealth and influence to help conduct slaves to freedom in the North and in Canada over the escape network known as the Underground Railroad.

In Ohio, a few months later, Weld's stagecoach was driven through a normally safe and shallow river. The melting snow of spring in 1832 had, however, turned the waterway into a torrent. But the drivers attempted the crossing anyway, and the horses and coach were swept downstream. Weighed down by his heavy boots and overcoat, Weld nearly drowned. He managed to pull himself out of the water, and nearby residents heard his cries for help. He later wrote this about the terrifying event:

> *I was surrounded by the horses rearing upon each other in panic and desperation of drowning frenzy.*

A Mission to Change Minds

After one of his travels, Weld reported to the Tappan brothers that Lane Theological Seminary in Cincinnati, Ohio, would be an ideal western location where young students could train for the ministry and do manual labor. In 1833, Weld enrolled at Lane, and he inspired a group of Oneida students to go with him. Although he was a student, he was known as a powerful speaker and was considered a leader at the school.

Secretly, he wanted to introduce his anti-slavery agenda to the students, many of whom came from slave states. Most of Lane's faculty and students believed slaveholders' arguments that "immediatism"— the immediate abolition of slavery—would disrupt American society. They also supported the position of the American Colonization Society (ACS). The ACS promoted the complicated and controversial plan to set up a "colony" in Africa in which freed slaves would settle. In an 1834 letter to Lewis Tappan, which William Lloyd Garrison published in his abolitionist paper *The Liberator*, Weld wrote of Lane Seminary:

> *A large colonization society existed, and abolitionism was regarded as the climax of absurdity, fanaticism, and blood.*

Weld felt he could change opinions like these by presenting facts. He wanted to discuss the slavery issue in public, but college officials prohibited students from discussing slavery. The students ignored the rules and organized a debate. The debate consisted of two questions and took place over 18 nights. One question asked whether slavery should immediately be abolished in slave-holding states. The other asked whether the position of the American Colonization Society was worthy of support.

The Great Slavery Debates at Lane Seminary

Students took turns presenting their case. The speakers included a student from a wealthy slave-owning family. He was convinced that slavery was a sin, and he explained the terrible effects of the practice. The only black student at Lane Seminary told his own sad story. He had been kidnapped as a child in Africa and then shipped to the United States to be sold as a slave. He became manager of his owner's plantation. Over many years, he worked enough in his spare time to buy his own freedom. He gave an emotional presentation on what African Americans wanted most: liberty and education.

At the end of the first nine nights, the majority of the audience voted in favor of abolition. For the next nine nights, the debate was over the settling of free blacks in Africa. Weld believed that blacks and whites should learn how to live together as free people. In the end, Weld's side won the debate and most of the audience voted against colonizing.

The Lane Rebels Move to Oberlin

After the debate, the students were inspired to create their own anti-slavery society and to begin working with African-American families in Cincinnati. During the summer, the students taught reading classes, created libraries, and offered other support to the community. The powerful white people in the city frowned on these actions, and they let the school know how they felt. When the school trustees asked the

Logic on fire... as eloquent as an angel and powerful as thunder!

– Lyman Beecher (shown here), father of author Harriet Beecher Stowe and president of Lane Theological Seminary, on the speaking style of Theodore Weld

students to stop their activities, Weld and more than 50 other students (known by then as the Lane Rebels) left the school in 1834.

Weld convinced the Lane Rebels to transfer to Oberlin College, also in Ohio. His friends Arthur and Lewis Tappan offered to make a large donation if the school promised to enroll white students and black students. School administrators agreed. In 1835, Oberlin became the first American college or university to regularly admit African-American students. Weld felt that at last he and his fellow students had a home where their belief in equality was supported. A few years later, in 1841, Oberlin became the first college to be coeducational, allowing women to study with male students and receive university degrees. Today Oberlin continues to embrace its reputation for diversity in its student population, its academic programs, and its policies promoting social justice on a variety of issues.

This illustration shows a group of African men, women, and children being captured by Arab slave traders. Most slaves were cruelly separated from their families upon being sold into slavery.

A New Society and New Challenges

Meanwhile, the Tappans were continuing their good work. They had formed the American Anti-Slavery Society (AASS) in 1833. The society became the strongest voice against slavery in the nation, inspiring like-minded people in other communities to start their own anti-slavery societies. The Tappan brothers also hired Weld as an agent for the AASS. His job was to convince people of the evils of slavery and to recruit others to spread the anti-slavery message.

Weld was an experienced traveler and speaker, but he would be facing much greater challenges and dangers after he became an anti-slavery activist. Mobs were waiting in every town to shout him down,

A New African Colony

The American Colonization Society (ACS) was founded in 1816. The ACS was the most prominent of several groups that devised plans for settlements of former slaves and other free blacks in Africa and on Caribbean islands. These settlements were known as "colonies." ACS supporters came from a variety of backgrounds and views on slavery. Some were members of white evangelical groups and Quakers, most of them supporters of the abolition of slavery. These people, along with some African Americans, felt that this migration was the best way to help black Americans gain true independence and freedom from an institution—slavery—that had rooted itself into American life, especially in the South.

When areas settled by freed blacks from the United States became Liberia, the citizens of that newly independent nation chose a design for their flag that bore obvious similarities to the flag of the United States.

Most of the support for the ACS came from whites who had other reasons for wanting to "colonize" Africa with freed blacks. These included white Southerners who feared that freed slaves would inspire revolts among other slaves in the South. Others were Northerners who feared that freed slaves would take jobs from white workers. Still others, while more sympathetic to African Americans, were not prepared to accept integration between blacks and whites. Others felt that freed blacks would not be able to compete in a free society. The ACS started a colony in Africa that became the nation of Liberia in 1847. By 1867, more than 13,000 freed slaves had relocated to Liberia.

A group of Liberian schoolgirls, photographed in 2007. Modern Liberians are a mix of native Africans and African Americans who settled in Liberia from the mid-1800s on.

and some resorted to rock-throwing and other kinds of physical violence. He persisted in the face of these threats, inspiring others to his side and moving anti-slavery crusader William Lloyd Garrison to call him "lion-hearted and invincible."

Weld had finally found his life's work. He no longer aspired to be a minister, but he would need all his preaching skills to change history.

Abolitionist Heroes

William Lloyd Garrison (1805–1879) was a leader in the anti-slavery movement. He was the publisher of the abolitionist newspaper *The Liberator* from 1831 until slavery was abolished following the Civil War. He helped found the American Anti-Slavery Society and supported the Union side during the war. Garrison also supported women's rights and encouraged women to become actively involved in the society. This stance caused disagreement among AASS members who were not ready to expand the vision of equality to include women as well as men of all races.

William Lloyd Garrison

Frederick Douglass (1818–1895) was born into slavery on a Maryland plantation. He learned to read and write after he was sent to Baltimore as a child. He later escaped from slavery, changing his name several times to avoid capture. A brilliant speaker, he lectured in Britain and Ireland for two years about the evils of slavery. After friends paid for his freedom, Douglass returned to live in the United States in 1847. His New York home was a safe house for fleeing slaves escaping to Canada via the Underground Railroad. Soon after his return to America, he began publishing an anti-slavery newspaper called *The North Star*.

A daguerreotype photograph of Frederick Douglass, taken when he was in his early 30s.

CHAPTER FOUR

Delivering the Message

As word spread about Theodore Weld's speeches, he earned a reputation as the finest orator of his time. In every town, after every speech, he signed up hundreds of new members to the American Anti-Slavery Society (AASS). Once people heard his compelling arguments about why slavery should be abolished, they were won over. Weld was so popular that often people were turned away from town halls already filled with people anxious to hear his message.

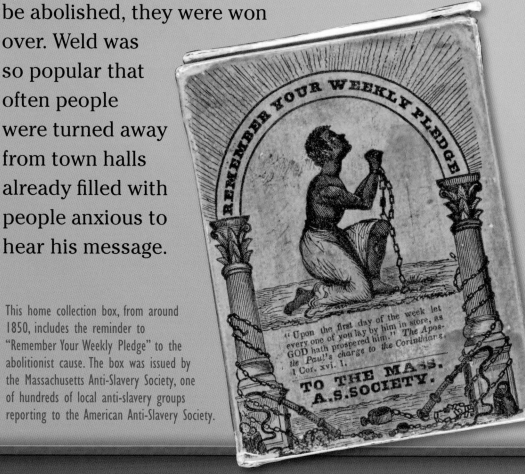

This home collection box, from around 1850, includes the reminder to "Remember Your Weekly Pledge" to the abolitionist cause. The box was issued by the Massachusetts Anti-Slavery Society, one of hundreds of local anti-slavery groups reporting to the American Anti-Slavery Society.

A Modest Man with a Powerful Message

Despite the power of his message and his gifts as an orator, Weld was a modest man who didn't like self-promotion. He didn't like to dress in grand clothes or go to parties. Many of his articles were written under assumed names, so his identity was kept secret much of the time. That may be why he isn't as well known as some of the other heroes of the abolitionist movement. As he once said of the first impression he imagined making on people:

> *I am a Backwoodsman untamed. My bearish proportions have never been licked into city shape and are quite too uncombed and shaggy for 'Boston notions.'*

Weld sought out people he could train as agents and lecturers for the new AASS. Among those he recruited were his former Lane and Oberlin classmates. Weld's agents were very successful at converting people among the general public. By 1835, 220 local anti-slavery societies were reporting to the AASS. A year later, there were 527 societies.

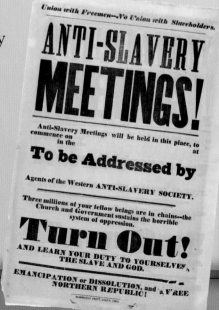

This poster was used to advertise anti-slavery rallies prior to the Civil War. Printed by a group following in the footsteps of the American Anti-Slavery Society, it carries language that shows the religious motivation of many abolitionists. It also expresses, in the following words, the belief that the primary abolitionist goal was gaining the freedom of fellow human beings, even if it meant breaking up the United States: "EMANCIPATION or DISSOLUTION, and a FREE NORTHERN REPUBLIC!"

From his early revival days, Weld knew there was anti-slavery support among churchgoing people. With those people in mind, Weld's new agents became known as the Band of 70, a reference to early followers of Jesus. Those followers, sometimes called the "the 70 disciples," were sent out to spread the word of Christianity nearly 2,000 years ago.

From Speeches to Essays

By 1836, the long hours of speaking and the constant traveling finally wore Weld out. He could no longer talk in the booming voice that was so inspiring to audiences. He decided the best way to help the anti-slavery cause was by writing. He worked for a time as the editor of a newspaper called the *Genius of Universal Emancipation*, also known as *The Emancipator*. Weld's influence shifted from rousing speeches to hard-hitting books and pamphlets. In his 1837 book called *The Bible Against Slavery*, he rejected the slave owners' belief that slavery was acceptable because it was mentioned in the Bible. Weld showed that their idea was "tortured common sense."

During his extensive travels, Weld met two exceptional women at an anti-slavery convention. They were the Grimké sisters, Sarah and Angelina, who had grown up in a slave-owning family in the South. When they rebelled against the idea of owning slaves, they moved North to become activists. Weld was inspired by their story and he, in turn, inspired them to lecture about abolition.

A New Cause and a Budding Romance

Weld worked with both the Grimké sisters and admired their devotion to the cause. All three of them traveled often, so they kept in touch by mail. He referred to them as his "dear sisters" in his letters. In their frequent messages to each other, they debated whether women's rights should be included in the fight for freedom for African Americans.

Gradually Weld's letters to Angelina grew more romantic, and he divulged his love for her. He wrote that he was still a boy at heart, and that he had a lot of bad habits. "I expect to cut all sorts of boyish capers

Crusading Women:
Angelina Grimké (1805–1879)
and Sarah Grimké (1792–1873)

Angelina Grimké

Despite growing up in a wealthy South Carolina family, Angelina (the youngest of 14 siblings) and her sister Sarah rejected the practice of slavery. As a child, Sarah had attempted to teach a slave how to read and write, which was illegal in South Carolina. Because of their beliefs, the sisters left the Presbyterian Church and became Quakers.

The Grimké sisters' anti-slavery activism brought them ridicule in the South, so they moved to Philadelphia, which had a thriving Quaker community. They toured in the Northern states to speak about abolition and women's rights. In 1838, they became the first women to speak to a state legislature in the United States when they made an anti-slavery speech before lawmakers in Massachusetts. They also challenged religious authorities on issues concerning both abolitionism and women's rights. Sarah wanted to become a Quaker minister, but her efforts fell short due to resistance from male Quaker officials. The sisters spoke and wrote against the notion that women were inferior to men. Their writings included two powerful pamphlets, "An Appeal to the Christian Women of the South," written by Angelina in 1836, and "Letters on the Equality of the Sexes," written by Sarah in 1837.

Sarah Grimké

with perfect zest," he wrote to Angelina. "I expect to be as long as I live just as much a baby boy as I was in the nursery."

Both of them were famous by this time, and their friends were surprised that two such strong personalities would agree to marry. Angelina was known as "Devil-ina" by the slave owners, and Weld's name was well known across the country. Their friends were excited

The *Amistad* Case

in 1841, a shipboard rebellion resulted in an important legal case that drew attention to the abolitionist cause. Kidnapped Africans aboard the Spanish schooner *Amistad* were being shipped as slaves from one location to another in Cuba, when they overpowered the crew and demanded to return home. Instead of heading for Africa, the ship was sailed up the U.S. coast, where it was seized by a U.S. government ship on patrol. Arguing that the Africans were "cargo" and should be sold, the Spanish government wanted them returned.

Abolitionists argued that kidnapping the Africans was illegal since the international slave trade had already been abolished. Former U.S. president John Quincy Adams defended the Africans, and the United States Supreme Court agreed that they were free to stay in the country or return home. The 36 surviving members sailed back to Africa with a group of missionaries in 1842.

Two artistic depictions of Senge Pieh, later known as Joseph Cinqué, leader of the Africans who took control of the *Amistad*, the Spanish ship transporting slaves from one port in Cuba to another. Right: A portrait of Cinqué shows him during a more peaceful time of his life, in Africa. Above: Cinqué is shown standing defiant in court. This scene is taken from "*Amistad* Mutiny," a three-panel mural painted around 1938 by African-American artist Hale Woodruff.

about the wedding, but they couldn't understand how Angelina was willing to start a domestic life with children, a husband, and housekeeping after she had been such a dynamic speaker and a supporter of equal rights for women.

The couple proved that marrying would not make them soften their opinions. Indeed, they chose to plan the wedding ceremony and their

> *Suppose I should seize you, rob you of your liberty, drive you into the field, and make you work without pay as long as you live, would that be justice and kindness, or monstrous injustice and cruelty?*

– From the Introduction to *American Slavery As It Is: Testimony of a Thousand Witnesses,* by Theodore Weld

legal married status in ways that would be more common today, but were very shocking to the conservative people of their era.

Their anti-slavery views were part of the plans for their wedding, to be held in Philadelphia on May 14, 1838. Angelina wrote the invitations herself on cards that featured an engraving of a slave in chains. They didn't ask a minister to conduct the ceremony. Instead, they made up their own vows and spoke them to each other. This was followed by prayers led by two ministers: an African American and a white man. They included freed slaves among the invited guests, surprising some people who were not used to seeing black people and white people socializing together.

While they believed they were equal partners in the marriage, the law at the time saw it differently. When women married, their money and possessions became their husband's property. Grimké was wealthier than Weld, and he rejected the law making her money his by stating from the start of their marriage that Grimké's property was her own.

They would spend more than 40 years together through hardship and happiness.

THE LASH.

One of a series of anti-slavery trading cards from the 1800s about the life of a slave. It clearly shows the brutal treatment of slaves by their owners. Pictures like this helped convince people that the cause of Theodore Weld, the Grimké sisters, and other abolitionists was just.

Before the Welds could settle into their new life together in New Jersey, they had to face more violent mobs determined to destroy the abolitionist movement. In Philadelphia, on May 14, 1838—the same day Theodore Weld and Angelina Grimké were married—an important new building was opened. Using donations from abolitionist supporters, the new Pennsylvania Hall was built as a place where people could gather to talk about controversial issues.

Anti-slavery groups were often turned away from churches and town halls because their speeches usually brought angry protesters. Angelina, Theodore, and people who supported their views, therefore welcomed the building as a valuable meeting place.

Abolition and Women's Rights

The first group to use the new Pennsylvania Hall was the Anti-Slavery Convention of American Women. Over several days, many of the most famous abolitionist leaders, including William Lloyd Garrison and Angelina Grimké Weld, spoke to the crowd. Outside, the opponents grew more violent. Only four days after the hall opened, an anti-abolitionist mob stormed the building and burned it to the ground.

Although none of their disagreements were as violent as the fury unleashed during the burning of Pennsylvania Hall, abolitionists had their share of disputes within the movement as well. Many members of the American Anti-Slavery Society held radical views that other abolitionists did not support. The more radical members included women and others active on AASS committees. They supported women's rights on several issues, particularly voting rights. They also believed that the United States Constitution, in its ignoring of the rights

Only days after Pennsylvania Hall opened to a meeting of the Anti-Slavery Convention of American Women in 1838, a pro-slavery mob attacked the building and set it on fire. Over the next few days, the mob's violence spread to other targets, including an African-American church and an orphanage for African-American children.

The cover of a program for a parade promoting the cause of women's suffrage, or voting rights. From the early days of the movement for women's rights, parades were often held to publicize the demand for equal treatment in society and under the law. Activists believed that holding parades and other public events would dramatize the ability of women to live and thrive in public places. In a culture deeply rooted in the idea that "a woman's place is in the home," this was a major challenge!

of African Americans, was essentially a pro-slavery document. Members holding these views were opposed by AASS members who wanted to work with, not against, the U.S. government to abolish slavery.

Split with Evangelical Supporters

Equal rights for women was an issue that also split religious groups backing the abolition movement. A woman speaking in public to an audience that included men was something that many people thought was indecent. Speaking out in any way was frowned upon. For example, a few years earlier, Angelina wrote a letter to the abolitionist newspaper *The Liberator*, and it was published. The members of her Quaker community in Philadelphia disapproved. Angelina had to choose her anti-slavery work over her obedience to her religion.

The masthead of William Lloyd Garrison's anti-slavery newspaper *The Liberator*. Angelina Grimké was a frequent contributor to the paper. Despite the forward thinking of its readers, many abolitionists felt that the paper should focus solely on anti-slavery causes and not include issues related to women's rights.

Weld believed in women's equality, but he believed the fight for rights would be more effective if they concentrated on abolishing slavery first. In one letter to the Grimké sisters, he wrote,

> *Let us all first wake up the nation to lift millions of slaves of both sexes from the dust, and turn them into MEN and then when we all have our hand in, it will be an easy matter to take millions of females from their knees and set them on their feet, or in other words transform them from babies into women.*

Angelina wrote back to Weld and argued that she couldn't work effectively for the anti-slavery movement when people didn't respect her. "How can we expect to be able to hold meetings much longer when people are so diligently taught to *despise us* for thus stepping out of the 'sphere of woman!'" she wrote. For decades, even within the abolitionist movement, Angelina and her colleagues in the women's movement found themselves arguing the case for linking women's rights and the freeing of the slaves. In one speech before an abolitionist group, Angelina said the following:

> *True, we have not had our hands manacled, but our hearts have been crushed... I want to be identified with the negro; until he gets his rights, we shall never have ours.*

Two views related to the auctioning of slaves. Left: A soldier sits outside a slave-selling business in 1864, during the time when Atlanta was captured by the Union during the Civil War. Right: This anti-slavery trading card depicts the cruel separation of a family at the time of their sale as slaves. Scenes like this had a powerful effect on people who might have been shielded from the horrors of slavery. They were vividly described in Theodore Weld's influential collection of firsthand reports on slavery, *American Slavery As It Is: Testimony of a Thousand Witnesses*.

American Slavery As It Is:
A Powerful Voice Against Bondage

While all the political upheavals were going on, the Welds retreated from the fray and set up house in Fort Lee, New Jersey, following their wedding in 1838. They also asked Angelina's sister Sarah to live with them. She had always been very close to Angelina and was unmarried, so it seemed natural that they include her in their family. She lived in their household for the rest of her life.

It wasn't long before the Welds started a family. They would eventually have three children: Charles Stuart, born in 1839; Theodore, born in 1841 and nicknamed "Sody"; and Sarah, born in 1844. Sadly, Sody developed a condition that forced the family to place him in a mental institution.

Weld had given up making speeches, so he devoted himself to putting together a work that would become the most influential book in the anti-slavery movement. Published in 1839, the book was called *American Slavery As It Is: Testimony of a Thousand Witnesses*. It consists of firsthand accounts by preachers, lawyers, and other respected people of what they saw of the treatment of slaves. It was Weld's idea that readers needed proof of these atrocities. Angelina and Sarah assisted Weld, spending six months researching newspaper articles and other sources that provided proof of the mistreatment of slaves. The book was intended to shock its readers into realizing how terrible the lives of slaves really were. For people in the North who were unfamiliar with slavery, the stories in the book made powerful ammunition for the abolitionists.

Refusing to Be Gagged

To win the battle against slavery, Weld knew he had to do more than earn public sympathy. He had to make slavery an issue that politicians must face. One tactic his group used was to create petitions signed by thousands of people, then present the documents to the government. His goal of forcing elected representatives to discuss and debate slavery was thwarted, however, when the United States House of Representatives passed a gag rule in 1836. The rule, which had been pushed through the House by representatives from Southern states,

From the Preface to American Slavery As It Is

We will prove that the slaves in the United States are treated with barbarous inhumanity; that they are overworked, underfed, wretchedly clad and lodged, and have insufficient sleep; that they are often made to wear round their necks iron collars armed with prongs, to drag heavy chains and weights at their feet while working in the field, and to wear yokes, and bells, and iron horns; that they are often kept confined in the stocks day and night for weeks together, made to wear gags in their mouths for hours or days, have some of their front teeth torn out or broken off, that they may be easily detected when they run away; that they are frequently flogged with terrible severity, have red pepper rubbed into their lacerated flesh, and hot brine, spirits of turpentine, [etc.], poured over the gashes to increase the torture; that they are often stripped naked, their backs and limbs cut with knives, bruised and mangled by scores and hundreds of blows with the paddle, and terribly torn by the claws of cats, drawn over them by their tormentors; that they are often hunted with blood hounds and shot down like beasts, or torn in pieces by dogs; that they are often suspended by the arms and whipped and beaten till they faint, and when revived by restoratives, beaten again till they faint, and sometimes till they die; that their ears are often cut off, their eyes knocked out, their bones broken, their flesh branded with red hot irons; that they are maimed, mutilated and burned to death over slow fires. All these things, and more, and worse, we shall prove.

A daguerreotype photo of John Quincy Adams, taken in 1843, around the time he caused a stir by insisting that the issue of slavery be debated in Congress.

banned discussions or debates in Congress concerning slavery.

Leaving his family on the farm, Weld went to Washington for two years to work with former U.S. president John Quincy Adams and other politicians against the gag rule. Following his single term as president (1825–1829), Adams was elected to Congress. Refusing to obey the gag rule, Adams kept introducing anti-slavery petitions into the House. His persistence angered his enemies in Congress. In 1842, they agreed to hold a debate on whether he should be censured, or formally criticized and reprimanded, for not obeying the rules.

Washington was abuzz with the news that John Quincy Adams, a former president of the United States, might be censured by his peers. A debate was just what Adams wanted and he was glad to seize the opportunity to not only defend himself, but to force the subject of slavery into the debate. Adams spent two weeks talking before the House about his reasons for abolishing slavery. Weld supported him by providing research and new ideas as fuel for the fiery orator. Weld also offered positive comments from the public to keep Adams' spirits high during the grueling contest. In the end, the House voted not to censure Adams. For many representatives, the purpose of this vote was more to put an end to the debate than to acquit Adams. Adams didn't give up the fight, however, and continued arguing for free speech until the rule was repealed in 1844.

A Nation at War with Itself

The anti-slavery movement even created its own political party—the Liberty Party—and nominated a candidate for president, James Birney. Losing elections in both 1840 and 1844, while Birney didn't win, the party

The Underground Railroad

To help slaves escape from the South to free states in the North and across the northern U.S. border to British North America (what would become Canada in 1867), abolition supporters created a network of safe houses and guidance along a route that was called the Underground Railroad. Escaped slaves fled by horseback and on foot. Supporters and "conductors" along the way hid them and led them away from border guards and slave hunters. If caught, the slaves would be returned to their masters, become enslaved once again, and most likely be severely punished. The network, which operated at its peak between 1840 and 1860, helped bring thousands of slaves to freedom.

The Underground Railroad was a network of people opposed to slavery who helped slaves escape to freedom in Northern free states and Canada. This painting by Charles T. Webber shows anti-slavery activists helping runaway slaves in Cincinnati, Ohio.

Harriet Tubman was an escaped slave who, as a "conductor" on the Underground Railroad, led more than 300 slaves to freedom. During the Civil War, she also served the Union cause as a cook, nurse, scout, and spy. In one remarkable display of bravery, she guided Union soldiers on a raid that freed over 700 slaves.

was able to spread its views to a wider audience. Anti-slavery voices began to be heard not just in meetings and in the halls of Congress, but in the campaigns of people running for political office. In the South, politicians and slaveholders held firm in their insistence that their states be allowed to determine their own course of action on the issue of slavery.

In only a few more years, most of the slaveholding states would secede and declare themselves a new nation, the Confederate States of America. Soon, Americans would become embroiled in an armed showdown, fighting a long and bloody Civil War. At the heart of the conflict was the issue of slavery and the question of whether the United States would stand as a single nation living under a common set of laws, or be torn in two.

Flags of the Union and the Confederacy. Central to the Civil War, which was fought between 1861 and 1865, was slavery and the question of whether the United States would be a single nation or two. Added to these issues was the question of what, if the Union did remain whole, the character and identity of that nation would be.

Anti-Slavery Crusaders

James G. Birney (1792–1857) was a lawyer and politician born in Kentucky. He originally supported the idea of sending former slaves to a newly formed colony in Africa, in present-day Liberia. After hearing Weld's compelling arguments, however, he supported complete abolition rather than sending freed American blacks to Africa. He published a newspaper in Cincinnati called *The Philanthropist*, which was often attacked because of its abolitionist views. The Liberty Party, a group of abolitionists, picked him as its candidate for president of the United States in the 1840 and 1844 elections.

James G. Birney's father was a slaveholder, but his family wasn't entirely at peace with the practice of slavery. Throughout his life, Birney shifted his own position on slavery. Over time, and during the course of a long career as a politician and social activist, he grew increasingly opposed to slavery. He died in 1857, surrounded by his abolitionist friends Theodore Weld, Angelina Grimké Weld, and Sarah Grimké in a peaceful, wooded community in New Jersey. By the time of his death, Birney was convinced that the only way to put an end to the practice of slavery was to wage war against it.

Anti-Slavery Crusaders

Gerrit Smith (1797–1874) was a wealthy New York philanthropist, abolitionist, and politician who tried to help African-American families start new lives. He ran for U.S. president in 1848, 1856, and 1860, and was elected to the U.S. House of Representatives as a member of the Free Soil Party. After only 18 months in office, he resigned from the House in 1854 out of frustration with the Kansas-Nebraska Act, which left the question of slavery open for the two new states about to be admitted to the Union.

Smith donated small farms to black families to create an African-American settlement in the Adirondack region of New York state. In 1848, he financially supported a mass escape of 77 slaves in Washington, D.C., which failed when the escaped slaves were captured as they were sailing away from Washington. He was also one of the Secret Six, a group of Northern abolitionists that funded an 1859 attack on a federal armory at Harpers Ferry, Virginia (now West Virginia). The attack, led by militant abolitionist **John Brown** (1800–1859), was intended to capture weapons and arm slaves in a planned uprising of slaves throughout the South. The attack failed, and Brown was tried for treason and sentenced to death. Historians feel that the attack hastened Virginia's secession from the Union. It would therefore have been one of the events that led to the Civil War.

Gerrit Smith (above) helped fund an attack on a federal armory in Harpers Ferry, Virginia. The goal of the attack, led by radical abolitionist John Brown, was to arm members of a slave revolt that was envisioned as spreading across the South. The attack failed, and Brown was later tried for treason and executed by hanging, as were several of his followers who had participated in the attack. This painting (left), entitled "The Last Moments of John Brown," by Thomas Hovenden, is a somewhat romanticized impression of Brown being led off to his death, an abolitionist hero to some and a traitorous murderer to others.

CHAPTER SIX

Intensifying Hostilities, and a Great Victory

I n the 1840s and 1850s, hostilities between pro-slavery and anti-slavery Americans were growing stronger, and more violent. In 1854, Congress passed a law creating Kansas and Nebraska as territories (areas of the nation that did not yet have full rights as states). This law, known as the Kansas-Nebraska Act, stated that these territories could decide on their own if they wanted to become slave states or free states.

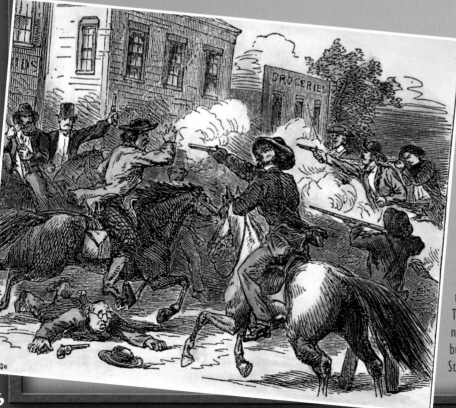

Lawrence, Kansas, was a hub of anti-slavery activity when pro-slavery thugs, known as Border Ruffians, attacked and ransacked the town in May 1856. The attackers smashed newspaper offices and burned down the Free State Hotel.

The Fight over Slavery Intensifies

Kansas became a battleground as people on both sides of the issue poured into the territory. Abolitionist settlers, known as Free Soilers, moved to Kansas from the East and Upper Midwest. Meanwhile, pro-slavery activists, called Border Ruffians, crossed the state line from Missouri to vote illegally and to intimidate Free Soilers. This period, between 1854 and 1861, came to be called "Bleeding Kansas" due to the many acts of violence that broke out in Kansas and neighboring towns in Missouri. Americans were riveted by Bleeding Kansas, and this period figured prominently in the build-up to the Civil War. Finally, just before the war began in 1861, Kansas joined the Union as a free state. The Nebraska Territory did not permit slavery, and its statehood came in 1867, after the war.

This 1856 map shows the United States following the passage of the 1854 Kansas-Nebraska Act. Free states are shown in pink, slave states in blue, and U.S. territories in green. A small "neutral" strip is shown in white. Kansas, where pro- and anti-slavery forces debated and fought over the issue of slavery, and Nebraska were still territories at the time but were eventually admitted to the Union as free states.

As the battle over slavery intensified, the work done by abolitionists like Weld in the 1830s had evolved into the actions of anti-slavery activists in the 1840s and 1850s. Weld's health had begun to weaken, and he had, in a sense, handed over the reins of abolitionist leadership as he worked on quieter pursuits of his own. In 1848, he started a small school on his 50-acre farm in New Jersey. He hoped that, through his teaching, he could influence a new generation. In 1854, he received an offer to run a coeducational school for students of all races in Perth Amboy, New Jersey. He accepted the offer, moving the whole family with him. He, Angelina, and Sarah taught at the Eagleswood school until it closed in 1862.

Steps Backward

African-American communities in the North grew, and managed to make a living on their own. Meanwhile, Southern landowners pushed their representatives in Congress to pass laws allowing them to reclaim their former slaves in states where slavery was banned. As a result of this pressure, Congress passed the controversial Fugitive Slave Act of 1850. The law forced

This photo of well-known abolitionists was taken at the 1850 Fugitive Slave Law Convention, an anti-slavery meeting held in Cazenovia, New York. The gathering was organized by Theodore Weld and other anti-slavery activists as a demonstration against the Fugitive Slave Act, which Congress was due to pass that year. The historic photo, taken by Theodore's brother Ezra, is one of the few known photographs of Theodore Weld and Angelina Grimké Weld (faces circled). The picture includes other prominent abolitionists, including renowned speaker and activist Frederick Douglass (sitting behind Weld), activist and philanthropist Gerrit Smith (standing behind Douglass), and Mary and Emily Edmondson (standing, wearing bonnets and patterned shawls). The Edmonson sisters were highly celebrated slaves who had been part of an unsuccessful attempt by 77 slaves to escape by sailing from Washington, D.C., to New Jersey in 1848. They were captured, but eventually they were freed by money raised by a church in Brooklyn, New York. They went on to attend school and campaign throughout the North for an end to slavery.

law enforcement officials to capture runaway slaves. Also under the law, people helping runaway slaves could be fined or sent to prison. The law further hardened the conflicting feelings over slavery on both sides of the issue. It also highlighted the conflicting interests and values of the North and South during what became the build-up to the Civil War.

An 1857 decision by the U.S. Supreme Court further inflamed abolitionists and others who were fighting the war against slavery through laws and in the courts. The ruling by the Supreme Court centered on Dred Scott, a slave whose master, John Emerson, was a U.S. Army doctor. After Emerson died, Scott attempted to buy his freedom from Emerson's

The Fugitive Slave Act

As the number of slaves in America grew, so did the number who tried to escape. In 1793, Congress passed the Fugitive Slave Act. A new act, passed in 1850, strengthened the law by making the return of slaves a federal rather than a state issue. It allowed slave hunters to get help from federal marshals when capturing escaped slaves in any state or territory, whether it be free or slave. It also provided for fines against officials who did not arrest runaway slaves. Suspected runaways would be taken before a federal judge, where they would have to prove they were not a slave. Most Northern states opposed the Act and did little to enforce it. Some states, such as Vermont, passed laws that challenged the federal law so they could protect freed slaves.

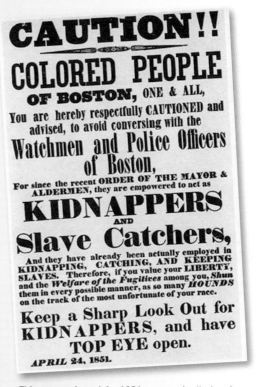

This poster, issued in 1851, warns the "colored people of Boston" that police officers may be acting as slave hunters.

Dred Scott's effort to win his freedom was denied by the U.S. Supreme Court when it ruled that slaves did not have the right to file lawsuits. The decision enraged abolitionists and others concerned over the rights of African Americans in free states and territories. It was effectively abolished after the Civil War with the 1867 passage of the Fourteenth Amendment of the U.S. Constitution. The Fourteenth Amendment requires states to provide all citizens with equal protection under the law, which includes granting the right, for those who qualify, to have U.S. citizenship. This newspaper from June 1857 displays portraits of Scott (lower left), his wife Harriet (lower right), and his daughters Eliza and Lizzie (above).

widow. When she refused, Scott went to court. Although Emerson and his slaves had moved to free states, Emerson had hired them out as slaves, which was against federal law. On this and other grounds, Scott thought he might have a chance at winning his freedom. His case worked its way up through various lower courts before reaching the Supreme Court, which is the highest court in the nation. In its ruling, known as the Dred Scott Decision, the court decreed that slaves did not have the right to bring a lawsuit to court because they were private property, not citizens. The ruling enraged abolitionists. It was also another sign of the increasing conflicts and tensions within a nation where some of its states and territories allowed slavery, while others were free.

In 1856, Charles Sumner, an anti-slavery senator from Massachusetts, was beaten by Preston S. Brooks, a pro-slavery representative from South Carolina, on the floor of the U.S. Senate. Sumner required three years to recover from his injuries, and Brooks received a relatively mild punishment. The passions fueled on both sides of the slavery issue by this incident are considered to be evidence of the mounting likelihood of the North and South going to war.

Out of Retirement

It was only a matter of time before these kinds of conflicts and battles—in places such as Kansas, in Congress and state lawmaking bodies, and in the courts—erupted into the Civil War. In 1862, William Lloyd Garrison, who had been so impressed with Weld's words and actions during the earlier days of the abolitionist movement, asked Weld to come out of retirement and give an anti-slavery speech at the Boston Music Hall. At first, Weld was concerned that his speaking voice would not be strong enough. Angelina encouraged him to go, and he was a great success.

In the pages of his abolitionist newspaper, *The Liberator*, William Lloyd Garrison argued fiercely and eloquently for no compromise on the issue of slavery. In his view, if it made no sense to allow slave states into the Union, it made no sense to allow slave states to remain in the Union. Even for Theodore Weld and other friends and fellow abolitionists, this position—the "dissolution" of the Union—was a radical one.

Only weeks earlier, President Abraham Lincoln had issued the first draft of his Emancipation Proclamation, which declared the freedom of slaves in any state that had withdrawn from the Union. Weld's speech, called "The Conspirators," was a timely attack on the lies of those who supported slavery. At the age of 59, Weld went on a speaking tour, which made him feel young again. For seven months, he spoke to crowds in Massachusetts, Rhode Island, New Hampshire, Pennsylvania, Ohio, and New York. In May 1863, his tour culminated in a speech before the American Anti-Slavery Society in New York City. In the same month, his wife Angelina spoke before another group—the Woman's National Loyal League, formed to promote progressive causes. One of the group's main goals was to convince Congress to adopt an amendment to the U.S. Constitution that would abolish slavery. In her presentation, Angelina stated the stark reality of how the moral character and identity of the nation was hinged on the passage of that amendment—and a Union victory in the Civil War:

> *The nation is in a death-struggle. It must either become one vast slaveocracy of petty tyrants, or wholly the land of the free.*

This photo, taken at a Union Army camp in 1862, shows escaped slaves in the company of Union soldiers. During the Civil War, many fugitive slaves fled to the Union Army, where they were called "contraband." This term was used to give the Union the authority to keep the slaves as "property" seized during the war, rather than return them to their owners in the South. Once the Emancipation Proclamation was issued in 1863, the Union had, by presidential decree, the right to declare the slaves free. At that point, many of them joined the fight against the Confederacy.

The Emancipation Proclamation and the Thirteenth Amendment

President Abraham Lincoln's Emancipation Proclamation, issued on January 1, 1863, freed most slaves but it extended only to the states that were in rebellion against the government—the states that had joined the Confederacy. Delaware, Kentucky, Maryland, and Missouri—all slave states that had stayed within the Union during the Civil War—were not affected by the Proclamation. Neither was Tennessee, which was under Union control; or West Virginia, which had broken free from Virginia and joined the Union in 1863 after deciding to gradually abolish slavery. The Proclamation was hailed and denounced for many of the same reasons. One of these was that, along with preserving the Union, freeing the slaves had become a main focus of the war.

The Thirteenth Amendment to the U.S. Constitution, which was approved by Congress in January 1865, before the end of the Civil War, freed all the slaves forever. It said: "Neither slavery nor involuntary servitude... shall exist within the United States." Before the amendment could become law, it had to be ratified, or approved, by three-quarters of the 36 states following the end of the Civil War. This occurred in December, when Georgia became the 27th state to ratify the amendment. Eventually, all states ratified the Thirteenth Amendment.

This print, produced in 1888 and titled "Abraham Lincoln and His Emancipation Proclamation," displays Lincoln's portrait surrounded by American flags and a bald eagle—the national bird of the United States. The Proclamation is flanked by figures representing Justice and Liberty.

A Victory, and More Work to Be Done

Weld and his family moved to Massachusetts in 1864. He was asked to help run another progressive girls' school in Lexington. There he taught moral training and the works of William Shakespeare, and Angelina taught history for several years. Weld's involvement in social causes slowed down again, but it did not end with the move to Massachusetts— or with the end of the Civil War.

With the North's victory in 1865, two historic goals were achieved. One was the preservation of the Union and the reunification of all American states and territories. The other was the end of slavery throughout the nation as a whole. In August of that year, just months after the Union's triumph, Weld went back to Oberlin College for a victorious reunion of his Lane Rebels and other students. Throughout the nation, however, huge differences in attitudes and beliefs regarding the rights of African Americans continued to divide people and states. Now that he had his voice back, Weld continued to be in demand as a speaker long after the anti-slavery movement had ended.

A man representing the Freedman's Bureau stands between armed groups of whites and blacks after the Civil War. The Bureau was formed in 1865 to aid newly freed slaves (known as freedmen) during the era after the Civil War known as Reconstruction. Bureau members helped African Americans gain an education and find family members from whom they had been separated under slavery. The Bureau also helped train African Americans for jobs and encouraged Southern plantation owners to work with blacks as employers and employees rather than as masters and slaves. These and other efforts to pull the nation back together proved to be far more difficult than imagined. For decades, bitter feelings lingered between North and South, and life for many blacks was as hard and dangerous as it had been under slavery.

Archibald and Francis Grimké

Archibald (1849–1930) and **Francis** (1852–1937) **Grimké** were two accomplished mixed-race men who succeeded despite racial prejudice both before and after the Civil War. The brothers were the children of Nancy Weston, who was a slave to their white father, Henry Grimké, the brother of Angelina and Sarah Grimké. In 1870, the brothers graduated from Lincoln University in Pennsylvania. Archibald went on to receive a law degree from Harvard University, and Francis received a graduate degree in religion from Princeton Theological Seminary.

Francis became a Presbyterian minister and community leader in Washington, D.C., and Archibald practiced law in Boston before becoming a diplomat and a civil rights leader. He served as U.S. consul to the Dominican Republic and later worked as vice-president of the National Association for the Advancement of Colored People (NAACP).

Francis had a daughter who died in infancy, and Archibald had a daughter, Angelina Weld Grimké (1880–1958), who became a poet, playwright, journalist, and political activist in her own right.

Archibald Grimké

Francis Grimké

Angelina Weld Grimké

Putting Their Moral Convictions to the Test

After the Civil War, Theodore and Angelina made a surprising discovery that would give them a chance to practice exactly what they had been preaching about for so long. In 1868, Angelina noticed an article about a black man named Grimké who had spoken at a Pennsylvania college. She was curious about a man who shared her last name, and she contacted him. To her shock, she discovered that he was her nephew. Her brother Henry had become involved in a relationship with one of his female slaves, Nancy Weston, after his wife Selina died in 1843. Henry and Selina's children were grown up, and he had another three children with Nancy—Archibald, Francis, and John, with whom Nancy was pregnant when Henry died.

Even though Archibald and Francis were Henry's own children, they were still slaves. Despite his devotion to Nancy, Henry had remained a supporter of the slave system. The laws in South Carolina, where Henry, Nancy, and their children lived, also made it very difficult for slave owners to free their slaves without going through a complicated legal process. Although Henry moved his family to a plantation outside of Charleston, where he could raise the children in relative privacy, he never freed them during his lifetime.

When Henry died in 1852, he left Nancy and their children in the care of his eldest son Montague. Henry said that Nancy and the boys should be treated like members of the family. Nancy, who was of mixed African and European descent, was given a place to live and the young boys attended school. They didn't get any financial support from Henry's other adult children, however, and Nancy worked to keep her family going. By 1860, Montague claimed the older boys as his slaves and brought them into his home to work as servants. When Francis resisted Montague's plans, Montague sold him. Fearing the same thing would happen to him, Archibald ran away and stayed in hiding until the Civil War ended. That is when the family gained their freedom.

When the Welds and Sarah Grimké met the young men, they realized that they had a duty to help these family members realize their great potential. They opened their home to the brothers and gave them money for their education. John eventually left school and returned to the South, where little was heard of him again. Archibald and Francis went on to graduate from some of the finest universities in the country.

The Later Years

As Weld grew older, he continued to speak out in support of the rights of African Americans and women. In 1870, the Welds led a demonstration on women's voting rights during a local town election. In a snowstorm, women and their male escorts marched to the voting station and

Women in line to vote in Seattle in 1911, the year after Washington state formally granted women the right to vote. Several states and territories granted women voting rights in the 1800s and early 1900s. In 1920, supporters of women's rights celebrated the passage of the Nineteenth Amendment to the U.S. Constitution, which granted voting rights to women in the nation as a whole.

handed in ballots. The women's ballots were not counted, as women weren't allowed to vote, but they held great symbolic value to those who believed in the equality of the sexes.

Sarah died in 1873. Weld took care of Angelina after she suffered a series of strokes. She died in 1879.

For the remaining years of his life, Weld continued offering his support to community causes such as the environment, a free library system, and women's rights. Until he was 90 years old, he also lectured on less controversial subjects that he was an expert on, such as education and Shakespeare. Weld lived with his son Charles for the rest of his life. Theodore Weld died at the age of 92.

A Great Life, and a Great Legacy

A humble and unassuming man, Theodore Weld did much of his writing anonymously or under assumed names. For this reason, many historians consider him to have been largely unrecognized as one of the most important and influential members of the movement to put an end to slavery.

Throughout his life, Weld worked tirelessly to create social change. Whether the issue was the abolition of slavery, women's rights, or curbing excessive alcohol consumption, he demonstrated a remarkable ability to rally supporters to the side that was, in his view, morally right. As much as

Americans take for granted racial equality and women's rights today, in the 1800s, Weld's views on these issues were years ahead of their time. His accomplishments are therefore all the more extraordinary because the causes he embraced were controversial and unpopular.

By presenting facts and rational arguments, Weld inspired other writers and teachers to defend human rights and to continue his work during the years when he retired from public life. As importantly, his writings, lectures, and actions helped convert thousands of ordinary citizens to the abolitionist cause. Unafraid of criticism and the threat of physical harm, Weld forced people to confront that which they did not wish to confront, to debate issues they preferred not to discuss, and to change views that no one had ever challenged. Weld succeeded at doing these things because of his own intellectual and moral courage, and his deep commitment to a belief in the rights of others.

This American postage stamp, issued in 1970, commemorates the 50th anniversary of the passage of the Nineteenth Amendment to the U.S. Constitution. The Nineteenth amendment granted universal suffrage, or voting rights, to American women in 1920. This amendment represented a victory for those who, like Theodore Weld, worked tirelessly, and in the face of violent opposition, for women's rights in the 1800s.

Chronology

1803 Theodore Weld is born November 23, in Hampton, Connecticut.

1819 Attends Phillips Andover Academy, private boarding school, but does not graduate.

1824 Returns from traveling the country giving lectures on mnemonics. Parents move to New York state. Attends nearby Hamilton College.

1826 Meets evangelist Charles Finney and becomes a traveling revivalist preacher.

1827–1830 Attends Oneida Institute in New York state.

1830 Becomes general agent for the Society to Promote Manual Labor.

1833 Enters Lane Seminary and prepares for the Lane debates on slavery; British Parliament passes legislation freeing 800,000 slaves in the Caribbean.

1834 When prohibited from anti-slavery activites, transfers from Lane with other students to Oberlin College. Hired as an agent for the American Anti-Slavery Society.

1835 Lectures on abolition.

1836 Loses voice and becomes editor for abolitionist newspaper *The Emancipator*.

1837 Weld publishes his first book, *The Bible Against Slavery*, an argument against using the Old Testament as a justification for slavery.

1838 Marries Angelina Grimké in Philadelphia on May 14. Three days later, the new Pennsylvania Hall, built by anti-slavery groups, is burned down by arsonists.

1839 Son Charles Stuart Weld is born. American Anti-Slavery Society splits over disagreements about women's participation and political strategy. Weld's most important book, *American Slavery As It Is*, a compilation of testimonials collected by Weld with help from Sarah and Angelina Grimké, is published.

1840 Buys a farm near Belleville, New Jersey, and starts a school.

1841 Son Theodore Grimké Weld is born.

1842 John Quincy Adams brings anti-slavery petitions to U.S. House of Representatives; colleagues debate on whether to censure him. Weld assists with Adams' research.

1844 Daughter Sarah Grimké Weld is born.

1850 Fugitive Slave Act passed.

1852 *Uncle Tom's Cabin*, a novel by Harriet Beecher Stowe, is published. Its anti-slavery message was inspired by Weld's book.

1854 Kansas-Nebraska Act is passed; allows states to decide for themselves about slavery.

1859 John Brown leads abolitionist attack on U.S. armory at Harpers Ferry, Virginia.

1860 Abraham Lincoln elected U.S. president. Southern states secede from Union to form Confederate States of America.

1861 Southern troops attack Fort Sumter, South Carolina, starting Civil War.

1862 Weld invited by abolitionist leader William Lloyd Garrison to speak at Boston Music Hall, ending retirement from public lecturing.

1863 President Lincoln issues Emancipation Proclamation, declaring freedom of most slaves in Confederacy.

1864 Weld family moves to Hyde Park, Massachusetts; Weld begins teaching at a girls' school.

1865 Civil War ends and, with it, slavery; Lincoln assassinated.

1873 Angelina's sister Sarah dies.

1879 Angelina dies; Weld lives with son Charles.

1895 Dies on February 3.

One of the few known photographs of Theodore Weld and Angelina Grimké Weld (faces circled), taken with other prominent abolitionists at the 1850 Fugitive Slave Law Convention in upstate New York.

abolitionist A person dedicated to ending, or abolishing, the practice of slavery.

amendment A change made to the original U.S. Constitution. For example, the Thirteenth Amendment abolished slavery.

armory A place where weapons are kept, usually by the military.

Border Ruffians Heavily armed pro-slavery forces who crossed the border from Missouri into the Kansas Territory.

censure Strong disapproval or criticism.

colonization Sending groups of settlers to a place and establishing control over that place. Colonizing a region may also include establishing control over native people who live there.

controversial Causing disagreement or argument.

convert To change one's religious faith or other beliefs.

daguerreotype Considered the first form of photography; invented by Louis Daguerre in 1839.

debate A formal argument that involves two people presenting opposing opinions on an issue.

emancipation Freedom.

evangelical Having to do with a passionate conversion or commitment to Christianity. The Second Great Awakening was a major evangelical movement in the 1800s.

free blacks The term used to describe African Americans who were not slaves during the period prior to the abolition of slavery.

legislature The branch of government that has the power to make laws; a group of people elected or chosen for that purpose.

mob An uncontrolled and unpredictable group of people.

moral Good or honest, having to do with what is right, not wrong.

obedience The willingness to carry out orders from an authority.

orator A skilled public speaker.

philanthropist A person who seeks to further the well-being of others, especially by donating money to good causes.

preach To deliver a message to others, usually a religious message in the form of a sermon.

race A classification of humans, usually by physical features.

radical Favoring extreme or very unusual changes.

rambunctious Wild or unruly.

ritual A series of actions that have symbolic value (as in a church service).

salvation Saving or delivering from the consequences of sin, usually through religious practices and beliefs.

secede To withdraw, or break away, from a group or an organization.

sermon A speech that offers inspiration or advice, such as one that might be delivered by a minister in a church.

suffrage The right to vote.

temperance Controlling or banning the drinking of alcoholic beverages.

theological Having to do with the study of God and religious belief.

Underground Railroad The secret network of people who helped slaves escape from the South to the North and into Canada.

An undated photo showing a celebration of the Emancipation Proclamation in Massachusetts. Featured in the photo are a crowd of civilians, a Union Army band and, according to an old tradition of the time, an honored person—in this case, an African-American man seated in a wheelbarrow (right).

Books

Bordewich, Fergus. *Bound for Canaan: The Epic Story of the Underground Railroad.* HarperCollins, 2005.

Hamilton, Virginia. *Many Thousands Gone: African Americans from Slavery to Freedom.* Knopf Books for Young Readers, 2002.

Press, David P. *Abraham Lincoln: The Great Emancipator* (Voices for Freedom: Abolitionist Heroes). Crabtree Publishing, 2013.

Stanchak, John. *Civil War* (DK Eyewitness Books). DK Publishing, Inc., 2000.

Thomas, William David. *William Lloyd Garrison: A Radical Voice Against Slavery* (Voices for Freedom: Abolitionist Heroes). Crabtree, 2009.

Websites

http://docsouth.unc.edu/neh/weld/weld.html
Documenting the American South is a comprehensive resource of teaching aids and primary documents collected and presented by the University of North Carolina at Chapel Hill. This link features the full text, in digital format, of Theodore Weld's influential work, *American Slavery As It Is: Testimony of a Thousand Witnesses.*

http://besthistorysites.net/index.php/american-history/1800/south-slavery
This site, part of a larger website called *Best of History Websites,* is designed for both teachers and students. It provides links to a wealth of information on slavery in America. Check out profiles of slaves living in both northern and southern communities. Listen to the voices of former slaves in "American Slave Narratives."

www.theliberatorfiles.com
Subscribe to *The Liberator!* This site has hundreds of articles from William Lloyd Garrison's newspaper arranged by year and by subject. The site also includes biographical information, some of Garrison's letters, a photo gallery, and more.

www.nationalgeographic.com/railroad/j1.html
Travel the Underground Railroad! Find out about the road to freedom at this interactive website. It features history, people, a virtual journey where you must make decisions that could lead to freedom or captivity, plus timelines, a map of possible routes, a "Did You Know?" section, and lots more.

Videos

American Experience: The Abolitionists (DVD). PBS, 2013.

American Experience: Reconstruction: The Second Civil War (DVD). PBS, 2005.

Index

Index

About the Author

Susan Brophy Down is an award-winning newspaper and magazine writer. She has covered a variety of topics such as business, arts and culture, and design.